Random Thoughts

Random Thoughts

thoughts and musings
by
Aline Talatinian

Originally published in 2008

Copyright © 2008 - 2014 Aline Talatinian
All rights reserved

Copenhagen, January 2014

Poems and photography © Aline Talatinian
Book design by Aline Talatinian

alinetalatinian.com

ISBN 978-87-992870-2-4

Contents

Tea in bed	3
Juste après	5
Information Overload	7
Mass Media	9
Separation devices	11
Random thoughts	12
Revelation	17
One and the same	19
If I could make money...	21
About me	22

Tea in bed

Woke up this morning
birds chirping in my head
you turned, kissed me
then jumped out of bed.

"Can I get you tea", you said
"I'll bring it to you in bed."
Can't you see
what I'd rather have instead

I tried to hold you back
but you slithered away
I wanted to tell you
stay please stay
but all I heard was "tea right away?"

Sank my face in the pillow
and tried to play dead
my body was aching
not for bread
All it would get
was tea in bed.

You came with the tea
pecked my cheek and smiled at me
for a moment I could see
my hopes turning to reality.

But again you turned away
leaving me there bare with despair
all I got was tea in bed
not before, not after, but instead.

Juste après

Les draps sont froissés
les jus séchés
le lit refroidi
les membres languis
le chant des oiseaux a remplacé
Les gémissements sans bruit
la réspiration relaxée
les doigts déliés
Le sourire aux lèvres
et dans l'âme
Les désirs sont assouvis.

Information Overload

With all those books to read
all the newspapers
the Google hits
All the podcasts
the blogs
the ingredient lists
All the radio shows
the interviews
the T.V. Talks
My father's words
my mother's looks
and the gossip heard

All the warning signs
instruction lists
and info kits...

Will I get wiser
or just overload my wits?

Mass Media

Media oh mass media

You tell me I'm naughty
when I'm good

You tell me I should be worried
when I'm happy

You say the world is a dangerous place
and I should be afraid

That problems are everywhere
Always

You say that if I prosper
I must be dishonest

and whoever is not like me
is my enemy

You say you reflect me
but I feel so misled

Media oh messy media
stop messing with me!

Separation devices

I'm here
you're there

not far
only two meters away

You have your screen
I have mine

our not so secret vices
our separation devices

Random thoughts

She's smiling
her little hand in mine
the world is good

The water was blue
Splash!
   She popped back up and smiled.

The phone rings
I drop my life
to take care of another's

He said
let there be this
there was this
Let there be that
there was that
That's how divinely simple
life can be

Drip drip
drops
A dog hops
Hiss
A snake
Oops
Too late!

Aging is like good cheese
You become stronger
mellower
        ...and smellier

Smile
and the world smiles to you
Don't laugh
It's true

Sweet eyes sweet nose sweet smile
A rogue cough from her little chest
My heart sinks

It's dark. The lights sparkle
The earth wet with just stopped rain
I feel peace.

My eyes mesmerized at the flame
there are no thoughts, no tomorrow, no past
still time. Only now...

Être maître
de tout son être
se laisser aller peut-être
sans apparaître
de renaître
comme un autre être.

Black sea
blinking lights
There's eight of them today.
Fishermen.

Time
goes by
You
stay dry
I
just sigh!

Each and every soldier said
No
I will not.
And that was the end of war.

Revelation

I peak into this
vast, bright and airy room
and the words
are floating around.
Suddenly I am inside
floating too.
I have been exposed
to the elements I need
All I have to do now
is take the words down
one by one
put them in the right order
and read the meaning
of my life.

One and the same

Atoms
millions of them
in clusters
out of clusters
darting
reaching
mingling
pulsating
filling space
filling Time
everywhere
all at once
it's you
it's me
The same.

If I could make money...

Why can't I ?
      Can't I ?

              Or won't I ?
                      Why won't I ?

What's stopping me?

A block on my way

so tiny
  I can't put my finger on it

so huge
  I can't get past it

so thin
  I could probably blow it away

If only I
 If only I
 If only I
      If only I knew what it was...

About me

Born somewhere, grown somewhere else, wandered here and there, now living elsewhere, I am working on accepting being where I am.

In the meantime, I lose myself in the moment when I try to capture the magic that reveals itself through the ordinary, if only we are open to see it.

Aline Talatinian.

www.ingramcontent.com/pod-product-compliance
Lightning Source LLC
Chambersburg PA
CBHW041814040426

42450CB00004B/155